DATES FRUIT

Amazing health benefits of dates for Body, Skin and Hair.

Table of contents

Introduction

Dates are a member of the palm family, flowering plant species mostly cultivated for its delicious fruit.

Phoenix dactylifera is the botanical name of date. It originated in Iraq. The leaves of the date tree are 4 to 6 meters in length, with spines of about 150 leaflets. The seeds can be used for animal feeds when it is grounded.

Fresh dates can be found from the months of August to December; however, dried dates can be bought any time of the year. For about 50 million years, date palms have been in existence.

In the Middle East and Indus valley, date fruit has been the staple food.

Dates are a very rich source of vitamins and minerals.

Chapter one

Nutrients in Dates

The following are nutrients contained in dates:

*Protein 1.81g 3%
*Energy 277 Kcal 14%
*Cholesterol 0 mg 0%
*Carbohydrates 74.97 g 58%
*Dietary Fiber 6.7 g 18%
*Total Fat 0.15 g <1%

VITAMINS

*Folates 15 µg 4%
*Niacin 1.610 mg 10%
*Pyridoxine 0.249 mg 19%
*Pantothenic acid 0.805 mg 16%
*Thiamin 0.050 mg 4%
*Riboflavin 0.060 mg 4.5%
*Vitamin C 0 mg 0%
*Vitamin K 2.7 µg 2%

ELECTROLYTES

*Sodium 1 mg 0%
*Potassium 696 mg 16%

MINERALS

*Calcium 64 mg 6.5%
*Magnesium 54 mg 13%
*Iron 0.90 mg 11%
*Copper 0.362 mg 40%
*Zinc 0.44 mg 4%
*Phosphorus 62 mg 9%
*Manganese 0.296 mg 13%

PHYTO-NUTRIENTS

*Lutein-zeaxanthin 23 µg
*Carotene-ß 89 µg
*Crypto-xanthin-ß 0 µg

A great amount of vitamins A, B6, and K can be found in dates. They help in the development of bones and improve eye health.

The fiber in dates improves intestinal health. It also prevents dangerous diseases such as cancer of the colon or stomach.

Minerals such as iron, calcium, protein, potassium, phosphorus, copper, manganese, magnesium, and sulfur help in the proper functioning of the body.

Dates also improve the metabolism and immunity of the body. Folate, can be found in dates; this nutrient is very good for pregnancy.

Niacin, thiamin and riboflavin are the other vitamins found in dates. These nutrients are good for proper cholesterol level, energy production and nervous system.

Chapter Two

Health benefits of dates

*It relieves constipation

Date pulp extract stimulates gastrointestinal transit activity; it helps in the treatment of constipation. This is achieved when the mineral content deregulation during constipation is corrected by the pulp of the fruit.

In a report released by the University of Rochester Medical Center, inadequate intake of fiber can result in constipation. Dates are a very good source of fiber and can put an end to constipation.

20 to 35 grams of fiber intake every day makes your stools become soft and also prevents constipation. It is necessary to limit the consumption of foods which lacks fiber.

*It improves your Heart health

A handful of dates a day are a great benefit to your health. Dates contain antioxidants; they prevent atherosclerosis.

Atherosclerosis occurs when the arteries get hard

and are clogged with plaque. Antioxidants stimulate cholesterol removal from the artery cells.

Dates also contain a great amount of isoflavones; they are known to reduce the risk of contacting cardiovascular disease.

Regular intake of dates reduces the risk of coronary heart disease. And also, the fiber in dates enables weight management, in order to avoid heart disease.

*It helps in Cholesterol regulation

Regular intake of dates can have beneficial effects on cholesterol levels and oxidative stress. Dates are very rich in iron and contain much fiber.

*It improves Bone health

Dates are rich sources of copper, magnesium, selenium and manganese. These nutrients are necessary for healthy bones and also they help in the prevention of bone-related conditions like osteoporosis. It contains vitamin K, which is a blood coagulant and metabolizes the bones.

*It helps in blood pressure regulation

The mineral, potassium, helps to lower blood

pressure levels. A good quantity of potassium can be found in dates. 167 mg of potassium can be found in one date, which is much higher than the potassium content in other fruit.

Kidney stones can be caused by inadequate consumption of potassium.

Harvard Medical School reported that the use of drugs for blood pressure regulation was strongly discouraged. Most of these drugs are known to have side effects.

Sugar levels are stabilized by fiber. The effect of sodium in a diet can also be counterbalanced by fiber which helps in lowering blood pressure.

Heart and blood vessels muscles are relaxed by the magnesium in this fruit; thereby reducing blood pressure.

*It improves sexual health

Date palm pollen is used in improving male fertility. Dates are rich in amino acids which increases sexual stamina.

*It treats Diarrhea

The potassium in dates helps to prevent and treat

diarrhea.

*It promotes brain health

Dates protect against brain inflammation and oxidative stress. Regular consumption of dates results in a lowered risk of neurodegenerative diseases and much better cognitive performances in elderly people.

It was concluded in a research carried out that supplementation of date fruits has the ability to reduce the progression of Alzheimer's.

Another research showed that dates prevent brain inflammation.

*It prevents colon cancer

Regular intake of dates prevents the colorectal cancer development. The consumption of dates increases the growth of beneficial bacteria in the gut. Dates promote the health of colon.

*It boosts energy

The date fruit contains several nutrients which help in boosting energy levels. Natural sugars like sucrose, fructose and glucose can be found in dates. These sugars offer a boost in energy.

***It promotes weight gain**

Add dates in your diet if you are thin and would love to add some pounds.

In a study carried out on lambs, a 30% weight gain was observed in the lambs after consuming ground date seeds.

*It prevents night blindness

Night blindness can be caused by deficiency in vitamin A. Dates are very rich in vitamin A. This nutrient helps in combating night blindness.

Night blindness is rare in regions where there is a regular consumption of the fruit.

*It prevents intoxication

In Northern Nigeria, dates and pepper are added to native beer to make the drink less intoxicating.

*It prevents hemorrhoids

Hemorrhoid is a common complication during pregnancy. Inadequate intake of fiber can cause hemorrhoid. Dates are excellent sources of fiber. They help prevent hemorrhoids during pregnancy.

*It prevents Inflammation

Date palms contain nutrients that fight inflammation. It also contains magnesium, which is a vital mineral for immune functioning.

When a diet is low in magnesium, which is common with most regular diets, your immune system will not be strong enough to fight inflammation.

*It supports healthy pregnancy

During pregnancy, a regular intake of dates is beneficial. Pregnant women require up to 300 calories more than non-pregnant women. Dates should be added to the diets of pregnant women. Dates are high in calories and nutrient-dense. Also, dates contain fiber which prevents pregnancy hemorrhoids.

The consumption of dates should be more regular in a month before labor; this strengthens the muscles of the uterus.

*It aids in anemia treatment

Dates contain a good amount of iron which helps to fight anemia.

*It promotes muscle development

Dates contain a good amount of carbs. The body tends to burn its muscles for energy when not enough carb is gotten. Dates, being high-carb fruits, might help in muscle development.

*It reduces belly fat

The fibers in dates help to reduce belly fat. Dates when eaten, makes you feel full quickly, thereby, discouraging overeating.

Also, since the dates are delicious, your sweet tooth is easily satisfied without having to opt for a less healthy alternative.

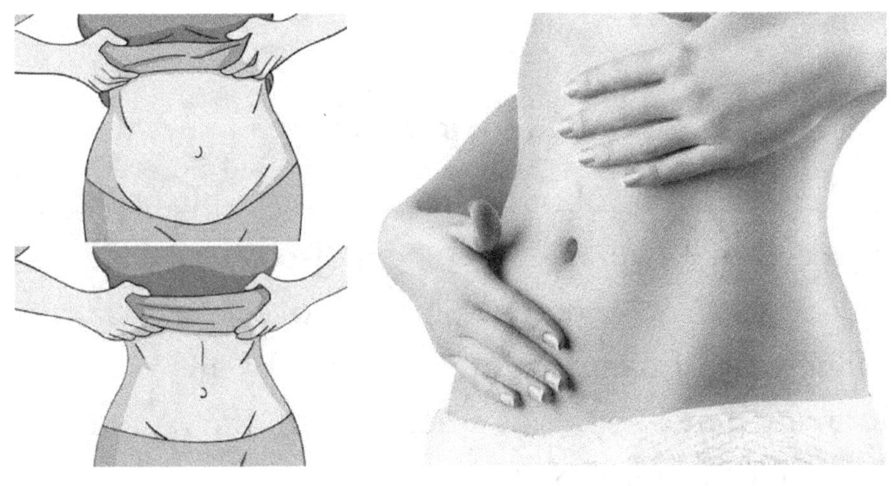

***It reduces blood pressure**

Magnesium helps to lower blood pressure. A high quantity of magnesium can be found in dates. Also, the potassium in dates helps the heart function properly and also reduces blood pressure.

***It reduces the risk of stroke**

After evaluating about seven studies published over a period of 14 years, researchers discovered that the risk of stroke was reduced by 9% for every 100 milligrams of magnesium consumed by an individual in a day. This research is in the American Journal of Clinical Nutrition.

Benefits of dates for the skin

The elasticity of the skin can be improved by Vitamin C & D found in Dates. The fruit can also help to fight various skin issues. A regular intake of dates has positive effects on the skin.

Also, Dates offer anti-aging benefits which prevents melanin accumulation in your body. The accumulation of melanin in the body has negative effects.

Date palm kernel extract contains phytohormones which reveal significant anti-aging effects. This extract helps in fighting wrinkles too.

Benefits of Dates for the hair

Dates are rich in iron and promote blood circulation to the scalp. It also promotes hair growth. Regular consumption of dates results in good blood circulation which causes oxygen to be released properly to your entire body including your scalp. This prevents unnecessary loss of hair.

CHAPTER THREE

HARVESTING

The date palm is a very old food-producing plant. It originated at the arid, desert regions of the Middle East, currently; it is grown in many parts of the world.

Date palm fruit can be harvested from September to early December.

Steps to follow when harvesting

Step 1

Wear thick leather work gloves and place the ladder (25 feet long) on the side of the date palm tree.

Step 2

Climb the ladder and wrap around a strand of dates a square of mesh netting. Use the pruning saw to cut the strand from the trunk.

Date stalks are usually 3 to 4 feet long, and wrapping the stalks in mesh netting a little larger than the stalks prevents any of the fruit from falling off when cutting through the stalks.

Step 3

Keep the stalks in a big plastic storage tub after coming down from the ladder. Harvest only ripe dates, which have a dark purple color with a shiny skin that is slightly wrinkled.

Ripe date stalks should be removed from the tree. Dates do not ripen together at the same time.

Step 4

From the ends of the stalks, pull out individual dates. Stalks should be discarded once you have removed all the fruit.

Keep the fruit on a cookie sheet, and then, set it in a cool, dry place.

Chapter Four

Preservation

Dates are preserved by cool storage.

Cleaning

Keep them on a screen tray or in smaller quantities, and rinse with a light spray of water. After that, place them in an environment where the temperature is 90 degrees F, allow them to air dry.

Dry dates should be kept in the refrigerator for eating or using in recipes within the next few days, weeks or months.

Dry dates can be kept for two or three months with no refrigeration. It can last up to eight months in the refrigerator. If you choose to put them in the refrigerator, seal tightly to prevent rehydration and spoiling from gases given off from other fruit.

Soft dates will not last for too long.

Unripe dates will last a few months longer than ripe dates; however, they will both last for over a year.

Cut pieces of dates into desired sizes or shapes and keep in a fruit dehydrator. Once dehydrated, the dates should be kept in a storage container.

Things You Will Need

>*Freezer bags
>*Screen tray or colander
>*Refrigerator storage containers

Keep dates in the sun for four or five hours, this will dehydrate them a little and give them longer preservation.

Put them in tepid water for rehydration, when you are ready to use them.

Conclusion

Dates are extremely beneficial to our health, with little or no money; this precious fruit can be gotten.

ABOUT THE AUTHOR

Mercy Obidake is a Writer, TV presenter and Blogger. She writes scripts for movies and Television programs, novels, articles and eBooks.

Aside from Writing, she enjoys providing humanitarian services to the less privileged in society. Mercy resides in Bayelsa State, Nigeria.